HOMES
in Different Places

Cynthia O'Brien

Crabtree Publishing Company
www.crabtreebooks.com

Learning About Our GLOBAL COMMUNITY

Author: Cynthia O'Brien

Publishing plan research and development: Reagan Miller

Writing team: Cynthia O'Brien and Crystal Sikkens

Editor: Reagan Miller

Notes to educators: Reagan Miller

Proofreader and indexer: Janine Deschenes

Design: Samara Parent

Photo research: Samara Parent

Production coordinator and prepress technician: Samara Parent

Print coordinator: Margaret Amy Salter

Photographs:
Shutterstock: © Muriel Lasure: title page;
    © Vadim Petrakov: p4 (left), p17; © IR Stone: p9;
    © Leonard Zhukovsky: p10; © Dmitry Chulov: p5 (top right), p18

iStock: © LifesizeImages: p6

All other images by Shutterstock

Front Cover: This colorful view shows houses and houseboats along a canal in the Netherlands.

Title Page: A family plays in front of a typical house in a village in Madagascar in Africa.

Library and Archives Canada Cataloguing in Publication

O'Brien, Cynthia (Cynthia J.), author
    Homes in different places / Cynthia O'Brien.

(Learning about our global community)
Includes index.
Issued in print and electronic formats.
ISBN 978-0-7787-2012-6 (bound).--ISBN 978-0-7787-2018-8 (paperback).--
ISBN 978-1-4271-1653-6 (pdf).--ISBN 978-1-4271-1647-5 (html)

    1. Dwellings--Juvenile literature. I. Title.

GT172.O37 2015   j392.3'6   C2015-903949-5
                                          C2015-903950-9

Library of Congress Cataloging-in-Publication Data

O'Brien, Cynthia.
    Homes in different places / Cynthia O'Brien.
        pages cm. -- (Learning about our global community)
    Includes index.
    ISBN 978-0-7787-2012-6 (reinforced library binding) --
    ISBN 978-0-7787-2018-8 (pbk.) -- ISBN 978-1-4271-1653-6 (electronic pdf) --
    ISBN 978-1-4271-1647-5 (electronic html)
    1. Dwellings--Juvenile literature. I. Title.

GT172.O37 2016
392.3'6--dc23
                                          2015025387

Crabtree Publishing Company

Printed in Canada/112015/EF20150911

www.crabtreebooks.com   1-800-387-7650

Published in Canada
Crabtree Publishing
616 Welland Ave.
St. Catharines, Ontario
L2M 5V6

Published in the United States
Crabtree Publishing
PMB 59051
350 Fifth Avenue, 59th Floor
New York, New York 10118

Published in the United Kingdom
Crabtree Publishing
Maritime House
Basin Road North, Hove
BN41 1WR

Published in Australia
Crabtree Publishing
3 Charles Street
Coburg North
VIC 3058

Contents

Our Global Community

Billions of people live in many different countries around the world. Each country is made up of **communities**. A community is a group of people that live, work, and play in the same area. Together, we all belong to one big community—the global community. We all live on planet Earth.

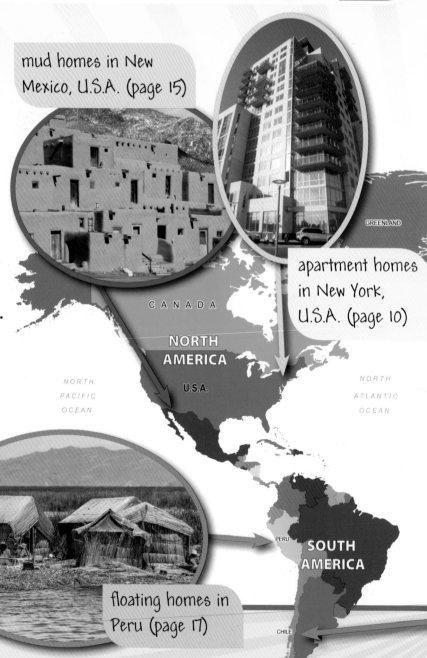

mud homes in New Mexico, U.S.A. (page 15)

apartment homes in New York, U.S.A. (page 10)

floating homes in Peru (page 17)

CANADA

NORTH AMERICA

NORTH PACIFIC OCEAN

U.S.A.

NORTH ATLANTIC OCEAN

GREENLAND

PERU

SOUTH AMERICA

CHILE

Different and alike

Everyone in our global community is connected. To find out how, we must learn how people live around the world. This will help us understand how we are the same, what things make us different, and the ways that we depend on each other.

Most people in the world live in a home. Homes come in different shapes and sizes. In this book, you will learn about the many homes in our global community. Take a look at some of them on the map below.

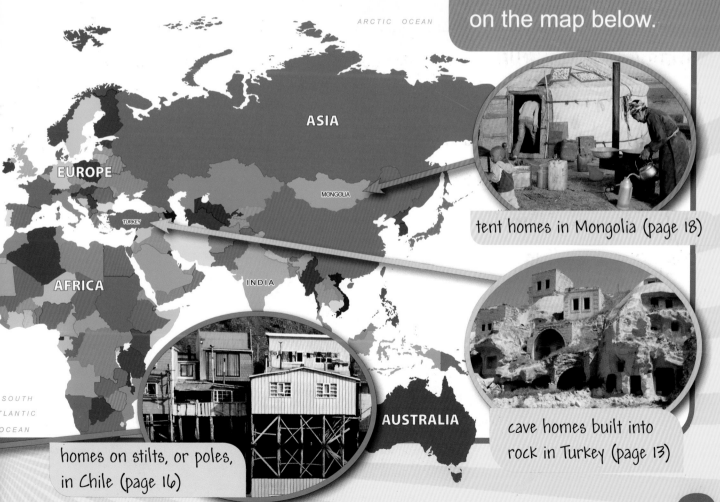

ARCTIC OCEAN

ASIA

EUROPE

MONGOLIA

TURKEY

AFRICA

INDIA

SOUTH ATLANTIC OCEAN

AUSTRALIA

tent homes in Mongolia (page 18)

cave homes built into rock in Turkey (page 13)

homes on stilts, or poles, in Chile (page 16)

A Basic Need

Homes around the world all have the same purpose. They provide a **basic need**. A basic need is something all people must have to survive. Homes provide **shelter** to keep people dry and safe. They also are a place to eat, sleep, and spend time with family and friends.

In a traditional Japanese house, people sit on mats on the floor to eat dinner together.

People that live in places with cold, snowy climates, build homes with **slanted** roofs. This helps the snow slide off more easily.

Meeting our Needs

The ways people meet their basic need for shelter depends a lot on where they live. The climate, or usual weather, in an area can affect the style or shape of a home. People that live in places with hot climates often build homes that have many windows. The windows help air flow through the home easily. This helps keep them cool.

Building a Home

The materials used to build a home change depending on the **environment**. Many homes are built using natural materials that are found in the area, such as wood, stone, mud, or grasses. Clay and dirt are common materials found in hot, dry areas. These materials can be used to build homes made of mud.

Mud homes are often built using mud bricks. The bricks are made from clay, water, sand, and straw.

Building materials

Grasses such as bamboo and straw grow in many rainy, **tropical** areas. Bamboo is a tough building material. It can stand up to strong winds commonly found in tropical areas. Rock or stone is one of the oldest building materials and can be found throughout the world. Rock homes, however, are hard to keep warm. They would not be a good choice when building a home in a cold climate.

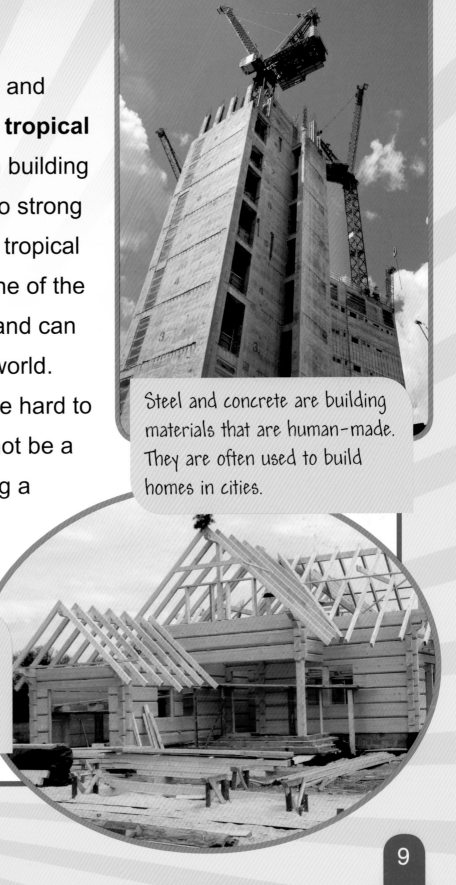

Steel and concrete are building materials that are human-made. They are often used to build homes in cities.

Wood is natural material from trees. Trees are found in many places. Wood can be used to build homes in most climates.

9

City homes

A city is a place where a lot of people live and work. Many people work in buildings, such as stores, offices, and factories. There are also a lot of homes in a city. Most **urban**, or city, homes are built close together. **Apartment buildings** are tall buildings that contain a lot of small homes. Thousands of people can live in one building! Townhouses are homes in the city that are joined side-by-side.

Over 8 million people live in New York City in the U.S.A. Many live in tall apartment buildings.

Many shanties built close together form a shanty town.

Large and small

Larger homes are often found in the suburbs. Suburbs are **neighborhoods** outside the city center, but are often still part of the city. In some countries, people may live in a shanty if they do not have enough money to live in a home in the city or suburbs. A shanty is a shelter in the city built with old materials such as cardboard, plastic, or metal. Shanties do not have electricity or running water.

Living in the Country

Rural homes are homes built in the countryside between cities. They may be in the mountains or on an island. Sometimes, these homes are far apart from each other. Other times, a small group of homes and other buildings may form a town or village.

A farm is a rural home. Farmers use the land around them to grow food or raise animals.

Living in caves

Some rural homes are built on hilltops or hillsides. Other homes are built into the land around them. Cave homes are built by digging into the side of cliffs or by digging underground. In Cappadocia, Turkey, people have lived in pointed hills of rock for thousands of years.

Entire towns have been carved into the rocks of Cappadocia. Many people still live in them today.

Cold and Hot Places

Homes in the Arctic are built with materials that help keep the heat inside. Most materials need to be brought to the Arctic by boat or truck.

The Arctic is an area located at the most northern part of Earth. It is cold for most of the year and the land is usually frozen. Homes in the Arctic cannot be built directly on the frozen ground. This is because the heat from the home can melt the land below and cause the house to sink and fall over. To prevent this, homes are built on short, steel poles dug deep into the ground. These poles keep the house steady.

Mud homes can last a long time. Some mud homes in New Mexico, U.S.A., are almost 1,000 years old.

Keeping cool

Homes in hot climates are built to keep the inside cool. Mud is a good building material for hot, dry areas because it helps to hold cool air inside the home. Thick walls and small windows also help to keep the heat out.

Homes on the Water

Many people live next to rivers, lakes, or oceans so they can fish for food or use the water for drinking and washing. In areas with heavy rain, the water level of rivers or lakes may rise and flood the land around them. Homes in these areas are often built on stilts, or poles. When the land is flooded, the water flows under the house and not inside.

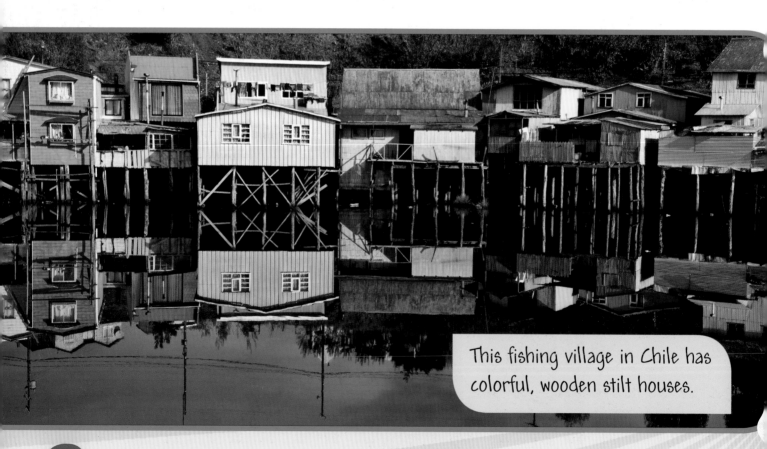

This fishing village in Chile has colorful, wooden stilt houses.

Lake Titicaca is located high in the Andes Mountains of Peru.

Floating homes

Some people live in homes that float on the water instead of living on stilts above it. On Lake Titicaca in Peru, native people known as the Uros live on 42 floating islands that were built using reed. Reed is a grass-like plant that grows in the lake. The Uros live in reed homes on the islands. They also move from island to island in reed boats.

On the Move

Some people spend their lives moving from place to place. They move in search of food for themselves and their animals, or for better weather. These **nomads** take their homes with them! The nomads in Mongolia live in circular tents called gers. Their tents can be taken down in just an hour and easily put back up again when they reach a new place.

Gers are made of wood or bamboo, and are covered with animal skins or felt.

Some houseboats, such as these in Jammu and Kashmir, India, stay in one place.

Houseboats

Fishers are people that catch fish or shellfish for food. Many fishers live on boats called houseboats. These homes can move easily in large lakes, rivers, or oceans. Some people live on houseboats for fun. These people might travel on houseboats to view the **scenery** and animals in an area.

Earth-Friendly Homes

Everyone in our global community needs to look after Earth. The materials we use to build our homes can help! Using **renewable** materials such as wood or bamboo are good choices because they can be replaced over time. Underground homes or homes built with grass roofs help hold in heat. These homes use less **energy** to stay warm.

Grass, or "living," roofs, like these in Iceland, have been used for hundreds of years.

Energy from the Sun

Using solar panels is another way to save our planet. Solar panels collect energy from the Sun and turn it into electricity. We use electricity to heat and cool our homes. Solar energy is a renewable resource. Solar panels produce electricity without creating harmful **pollution**.

Solar panels can be put on the roofs of houses and other buildings.

Notes to Educators

Objective:

This title encourages readers to make global connections by understanding that even though people around the world live in different kinds of homes, people use their homes to meet the same basic need for shelter.

Main Concepts Include:

- people use resources available around them to build homes
- people build homes to suit their climate and environment

Discussion Prompts:

- Revisit the homes described in the book. Connect each type of home to the climate or environment in which it is found. Ask readers how each home is suited for the climate or environment.

Activity Suggestions:

- Invite children to make models of a kind of home they learned about in the book. Provide supplies such as egg cartons, small cardboard boxes, paper rolls, construction paper, clay, craft sticks, tape, glue, and other available supplies.

- Encourage children to add as much detail as possible to their models.

- Once completed, invite children to present their model homes.

- Guide students by providing sentence starters such as:
  - I made a model of a _____ home.
  - This kind of home is found in: _____.
  - I used these materials to make my model: _____, _____, _____.

- Encourage children to point out the different features they included on their models.

Learning More

Books

Tate, Nikki and Dani Tate-Stratton. *Take Shelter: At Home Around the World*. Orca 2014.

Dustman, Jeanne. *Homes Around the World*. Teacher Created Materials 2014.

Lewis, Clare. *Homes Around the World*. Capstone 2014.

Websites

www.globaleducation.edu.au/teaching-activity/my-place,-your-place.html
This educational site includes many activities that promote global citizenship.

www.shelterpub.com/_wonderful_houses/wh-toc.html
This online resource features photos and information about different homes.

www.nlb.gov.sg/sure/wp-content/uploads/2013/11/Cheatsheet_house_Final_lowres.pdf
This site features eight different types of homes and includes information about where they are found and how they are built.

Glossary

Note: Some **boldfaced** words are defined where they appear in the book.

energy [EN-er-jee] (noun) The power, such as heat or electricity, used to make many human-made things work

environment [en-VI-run-ment] (noun) Everything that surrounds us, such as types of land

neighborhoods [NAY-bur-huds] (noun) Areas within a community where people live

nomads [NOH-mad] (noun) People who move from place to place and do not have a fixed home

pollution [puh-LOO-shuh n] (noun) Harmful substances, such as oil, that have been put into the environment

renewable [ree-NOO-uh-bul] (adjective) Able to be replaced, such as a tree

rural [RUR-uhl] (adjective) Having to do with the countryside

scenery [SEE-nuh-ree] (noun) The look of a place or landscape—usually beautiful or pleasant

shelter [SHEL-tur] (noun) A structure that protects from weather and other dangers

slanted [slahnt-ed] (adjective) To be sloped; on a downward angle

tropical [TROP-i-kuh l] (adjective) Having to do with a hot, humid place

Index

A noun is a person, place, or thing. An adjective tells us what something is like.